LEVEL

2

Ugly Animals

Laura Marsh

NATIONAL GEOGRAPHIC

Washington, D.C.

For the scientists and researchers
who spend their life's work helping animals
on our planet. —L. F. M.

Copyright © 2015 National Geographic Society

Published by the National Geographic
Society, Washington, D.C. 20036.

Trade paperback ISBN: 978-1-4263-2129-0
Reinforced library binding ISBN:
978-1-4263-2130-6

Editor: Shelby Alinsky
Art Director: Amanda Larsen
Editorial: Snapdragon Books
Designer: YAY! Design
Photo Editor: Lori Epstein
Design Production Assistants: Sanjida Rashid and
Rachel Kenny

The publisher and author gratefully acknowledge
the expert content review of this book by Sharon
Glaeser, research associate of the Oregon Zoo,
and the literacy review of this book by Mariam
Jean Dreher, professor of reading education,
University of Maryland, College Park.

Cover photo: king vulture; title page: pangolin

Photo Credits
MP = Minden Pictures; NPL: Nature Picture Library
Cover, George Cleminte/Shutterstock; 1, epa
European Pressphoto Agency/Alamy; 3, David
Tipling/NPL; 4-5, Birgitte Wilms/MP; 6, Jiang
Hongyan/Shutterstock; 7, Frans Lanting/National
Geographic Creative; 8, Tomatito/Shutterstock;
9, John Cancalosi/Alamy; 10-11, Frans Lanting/
National Geographic Creative; 12, Dembinsky
Photo Assoc./FLPA/MP; 13, Piotr Naskrecki/MP;
14, Orhan Cam/Shutterstock; 15 (UP), Tim Laman;
15 (LO), Andrew Snyder/NPL; 16 (UP), Pete Oxford/
MP; 16 (CTR), Sandesh Kadur/NPL; 16 (LO), Albert
Lleal/MP; 17 (UP), Stephen Dalton/MP; 17 (LO),
Daniel Heuclin/NPL; 18-19, Paul Nicklen/National
Geographic Creative; 20, Cyril Ruoso/MP; 21,
David Kearnes/Innerspace Visions/Seapics; 22,
Norbert Wu/MP; 23 (UP), Norbert Wu/Science
Faction/Corbis; 23 (LO), Kerryn Parkinson/NOR-
FANZ/Caters News/Zuma Press; 24, javarman/
Shutterstock; 25 (UP), Mark Carwardine/Photo-
library RM/Getty Images; 25 (LO), David Haring/
DUPC/Oxford Scientific RM/Getty Images; 26,
Ronald Messemaker/Buiten-beeld/MP; 27, Piotr
Naskrecki/MP; 28-29, Oxford Scientific/Getty
Images; 30 (UP-1A), Gerry Ellis/MP; 30 (UP-1C),
Michael and Patricia Fogden/MP/MP; 30 (UP-1D),
yzoa/Shutterstock; 30 (UP-1B), Lynn M. Stone/
NPL; 30 (CTR), Frans Lanting/Corbis; 30 (LO),
Chua Han Hsiung/Shutterstock; 31 (UP), NPL/
Alamy; 31 (CTR RT), Mark Carwardine/Photo-
library RM/Getty Images; 31 (CTR LE), image-
BROKER/Alamy; 31 (LO), Tim Laman; 32 (UPLE),
Nashepard/Shutterstock; 32 (UPRT), kajornyot/
Shutterstock; 32 (CTR LE), Albert Lleal/MP; 32
(CTR RT), Image Source/Getty Images; 32 (LOLE),
Art Wolfe/Iconica/Getty Images; 32 (LORT),
Dembinsky Photo Assoc./FLPA/MP; Top border
(throughout), EV-DA/Shutterstock; Vocabulary box
art, Val_Iva/Shutterstock

National Geographic supports K–12 educators with ELA Common Core Resources.
Visit natgeoed.org/commoncore for more information.

Printed in the United States of America
15/WOR/1

Table of Contents

tarsier

What Is That?

On the ground.
In the air.
In the water.

There are
ugly animals
everywhere.
These animals
might not be
pretty. But their
strange bodies
help them live
on Earth. Let's
find out how!

Q Why do some fish live in salt water?

A Because pepper makes them sneeze!

rosy-lipped batfish

On the Ground

You can find lots of weird-looking creatures. Try looking down near the ground.

The praying mantis gets its name from its front legs. They look bent in prayer. Yet those legs are used to hunt. Tiny spikes hook on to prey so it can't get away.

Critter Term

PREY: an animal that is eaten by another animal

praying mantis

tapir

Is it a pig? Is it an elephant? No, it's a tapir (TAY-pur)! A tapir's trunk grabs leaves and fruit to eat. It makes a great snorkel in the water, too.

jumping spider

Some jumping spiders can jump up to 50 times their own body length.

You can find this critter on the ground ... but not for long! A jumping spider spots prey with its eight eyes. Then it jumps on its meal.

On the short-horned lizard, spines warn predators to back off. If that doesn't work, it shoots blood from its eyes! The predator is surprised, and the lizard can get away.

Critter Term

PREDATOR: an animal that hunts and eats other animals

short-horned lizard

The blood tastes terrible to predators such as dogs, wolves, and coyotes.

Under the Earth

Some animals spend their lives underground. Their bodies are built for digging in darkness.

naked mole rat

The naked mole rat won't win any beauty contests. But its big teeth help it dig tunnels and find food.

Underground, it doesn't need hair to protect it from the sun. The few hairs it has act like whiskers. They feel things in the dark.

11

star-nosed mole

The nose on the star-nosed mole looks like something from outer space. But this nose is a big help on Earth. The 22 tentacles (TEN-ta-culs) can feel prey in a flash.

Critter Term

TENTACLE: an armlike part of an animal used to feel things or catch food

Believe it or not, a caecilian (seh-SILL-yen) is not a snake. It is an amphibian that does not have legs. Its thick, pointed head helps it make tunnels underground.

Critter Term

AMPHIBIAN: An animal that begins life in water and moves to land as an adult. Frogs and salamanders are amphibians.

Most caecilians have tiny eyes that are covered by skin.

caecilian

In the Air

king vulture

The king vulture's head can be red, orange, purple, and yellow.

When searching for strange-looking animals, don't forget to look up!

The ugliest part of a king vulture is its head. A vulture sticks its head into the dead animals it eats. Without feathers on its head, this bird stays clean.

A colugo glides through the air. Its stretched skin acts like a sail. High in the trees, a colugo eats leaves and stays safe from predators.

colugo

You can tell how the leaf-nosed bat got its name. Scientists think its special nose may be used for echolocation (eck-oh-low-KAY-shun).

Critter Term

leaf-nosed bat

ECHOLOCATION: A way to find objects by using sound waves. Bats and dolphins use echolocation.

5 UGLY FROGS

TITICACA FROG

At the bottom of Lake Titicaca, this frog stays away from strong sun rays and freezing temperatures. It breathes through all its extra skin deep underwater.

1

2

PIG-NOSED FROG
(also called Indian purple frog)

This crazy critter lives underground. Its short, strong limbs are used like shovels to dig up to 12 feet deep.

GOLDEN POISON DART FROG

This frog's bright color warns predators to back off. It has enough poison on its skin to kill ten humans.

3

4

WALLACE'S FLYING FROG

This frog's big webbed hands and feet work like parachutes. It glides through the air. Large sticky pads on its toes help it land safely.

5

AMAZON HORNED FROG

This frog hides easily among the leaves. When prey passes, it snatches dinner with its big mouth and sharp teeth.

In the Water

There are lots of odd-looking creatures in the water. The deeper you go, the stranger they get.

Near the surface, a male elephant seal has a nose that is big and ugly. The size and shape of its nose change the sound of its roar. Some scientists think this sound tells other males to stay away.

elephant seal

mudskipper

Mudskippers dig holes in the mud and lay eggs on land.

In the water, a mudskipper swims like other fish. Out of the water, it walks on land! Its strong front fins work like legs to carry its body.

A viper moray's long, thin body helps it hide between the rocks. Prey swims by, then ... chomp! The moray grabs it, then hides again.

viper moray

Deep in the ocean, there is little food. Some creatures have strange bodies that help them live there.

The anglerfish dangles a light from its head that looks like food. Prey comes closer. Then the anglerfish eats it.

anglerfish

22

A hagfish makes
its own slime—
lots of it. Predators
choke on it. They let go
of the hagfish in order to breathe.

The blobfish looks like its name. Its
gooey body helps it float above the
seafloor. It eats animals that float, too.

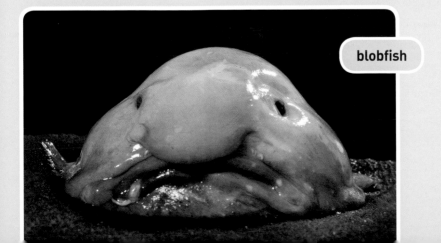

blobfish

In the Trees

Many interesting animals make their home in the trees. Do you know them?

aye-aye

The aye-aye (EYE-eye) has big eyes and ears. At night, they help the animal see and hear in the forest.

The aye-aye's long middle finger helps it eat. The finger works like a spoon to scoop out fruits and egg yolks. It scrapes bugs from the trees for a tasty snack. Yum!

A male proboscis (proh-BAH-sis) monkey's huge nose acts like a microphone. It makes the monkey's call sound louder.

proboscis monkey

leaf-tailed gecko

This kind of leaf-tailed gecko has red eyes, tiny horns, and speckled skin. All of these things help the gecko blend into the forest where it lives. This keeps it safe from predators.

In Outer Space?!

The water bear lives in water. It can live in very cold and very hot temperatures. Scientists have found that it could even survive in outer space!

water bear

A water bear is tiny. You need a microscope to see it. This photo shows a water bear much bigger than it really is.

Now you know that ugly animals can walk, swim, and fly all over the Earth— and even beyond.

QUIZ WHIZ

How much do you know about ugly animals? After reading this book, probably a lot! Take this quiz and find out.

Answers are at the bottom of page 31.

1

Which animal uses its nose as a snorkel?

A. proboscis monkey
B. tapir
C. praying mantis
D. aye-aye

2

The naked mole rat uses its teeth to _____.

A. find a partner
B. feel its way in the dark
C. dig tunnels
D. say hello to the neighbors

The king vulture's head with no feathers _____.

A. helps it stay clean while eating
B. scares away predators
C. attracts bugs it can eat
D. keeps it afloat in the water

3

4

The Titicaca frog has what strange body part?

A. a big tail
B. brightly colored skin
C. huge bulging eyes
D. lots of extra skin

5

How is the aye-aye's long finger helpful?

A. It scoops out fruit to eat.
B. It scares away predators.
C. It pokes other animals.
D. It makes a great magic wand.

6

Which animal has a light dangling from its head?

A. hagfish
B. anglerfish
C. viper moray
D. mudskipper

7

Where does the colugo stay safe from predators?

A. in the ocean
B. underground
C. in the trees
D. in caves

Answers: 1. B, 2. C, 3. A, 4. D, 5. A, 6. B, 7. C

AMPHIBIAN: An animal that begins life in water and moves to land as an adult. Frogs and salamanders are amphibians.

ECHOLOCATION: A way to find objects by using sound waves. Bats and dolphins use echolocation.

POISON: something that can kill or hurt other animals if eaten

PREDATOR: an animal that hunts and eats other animals

PREY: an animal that is eaten by another animal

TENTACLE: an armlike part of an animal used to feel things or catch food